ALL CHURCHED OUT

ALL CHURCHED OUT

Michelle Lynch

XULON PRESS

Xulon Press
2301 Lucien Way #415
Maitland, FL 32751
407.339.4217
www.xulonpress.com

© 2018 by Michelle Lynch

All rights reserved solely by the author. The author guarantees all contents are original and do not infringe upon the legal rights of any other person or work. No part of this book may be reproduced in any form without the permission of the author. The views expressed in this book are not necessarily those of the publisher.

Unless otherwise indicated, Scripture quotations taken from the King James Version (KJV) – *public domain*.

Scripture quotations taken from the New King James Version (NKJV). Copyright © 1982 by Thomas Nelson, Inc. Used by permission. All rights reserved.

Printed in the United States of America.

ISBN-13: 978-1-54562-923-9

DEDICATION

This book is dedicated to my readers, friends and family who have supported me in ways I would have never imagined. You all are the reason I have pushed even harder toward my destiny. This is an amazing journey, and I am so grateful to share it with you.

TABLE OF CONTENTS

DEDICATION v

FOREWORD ix

Chapter One	WHERE DO WE GO FROM HERE?	3
Chapter Two	NO ONE UNDERSTANDS	13
Chapter Three	CONTINUED FRUSTRATION	19
Chapter Four	THE WORDS OF A MOTHER	29
Chapter Five	NO GOING BACK	33
Chapter Six	REAL LOVE	37
Chapter Seven	CHANGES	41
Chapter Eight	GROWING PAINS	49
Chapter Nine	LIFE AS THE HUSBAND SEES IT	51
Chapter Ten	HIS EGO AND HIS HEART	57
Chapter Eleven	THINGS AS THEY SEEMED	65
Chapter Twelve	RIGHT OR WRONG?	69
Chapter Thirteen	A DAUGHTER'S ANSWERED PRAYER	75

FOREWORD

When you consider the church of yesterday, we were told that it was God first and everything and everyone else later, so we took our problems, situations, our families and dare I say our purpose and placed it on a shelf in order to fit into the body of Christ to do good deeds. After years of serving in the church, going to church every Sunday, Wednesday and Friday; pleasing the Pastor and the various people in the different ministries; believing that we are creating and maintaining relationships in the Body of Christ; that we are a part of and doing God a service, which will enable us a ticket into Heaven; we find that it was not what we thought it was.

The zeal and excitement we once had to get up and do the work of the Lord has turned into a life of drudgery and uncertainty. In this book, Michele Lynch has brought to life the reality of what it is that we thought was right; and enabled us to see that it was all a mirage. As a Christian, life can begin to feel as if we are running like a hamster on the wheel, but we attribute it as the Apostle Paul said, to "fighting the good fight of faith;" when faith had nothing to do with it – it was all about pleasing people.

Entrenched in this book you will find the way to live life to its fullest by putting your life in perspective and understanding the chain of command God wants you to follow. Walking in a life of total Freedom, Joy, Love and Happiness that leads to experiencing not only the true Joy of the Lord, but True Relationship.

–Min. Jacqueline Belcher
Abundant Life Family Worship Center
New Brunswick, New Jersey

    Many families are faced with the challenges of the differences in opinions, backgrounds, logic, and morals. The story of the Thompson family parallels many families across the country.

    Once upon a time, Angela and her husband, Rick, had it all figured out. Of course they've had their share of disagreements, but nothing threatened their relationship until Angela joined a church.

    This misunderstanding arose when Angela began to spend the majority of her spare time with her church family versus the time she had formally spent with Rick and their two children, Nikki and Tyler.

    The couple continued to push through the endless arguments, while their children watched them struggle to maintain a sense of unity.

    Just when Angela believed she could continue to maintain a wholesome relationship with her husband and children, they were faced with a surprise they had to face head-on, as a family.

    Rick handled things his way, and Angela handled things her way. The more Rick wanted Angela home with him and the children, the more Angela wanted to be in church, enjoying the much-needed validation and the escape from her emotionally tumultuous home life.

Angela and Rick's daughter, Nikki, noticed every moment of it.

God proved to the entire family that prayers never go unanswered, and He meets them right at their point of complete vulnerability.

CHAPTER ONE

WHERE DO WE GO FROM HERE?

The beautiful summer was upon us, yet there was a darkness that covered the place we once called home. The warmth of the sun couldn't even hold me the way I craved.

How could the summer feel so cold?

The love we used to have for one another, and the feeling of togetherness and family seemed to be a thing of the past. I doubted if the relationship my parents shared was ever real.

I thought back on the years when I believed we were all happy, trying to decide if this was all a charade, while Tyler and I sat and watched our parents fake it and fail.

A few weeks went by, and the cumbersome silence took its toll on all of us. The more I thought about it, the less I could concentrate on the rest of my life.

The time that I should have spent having fun with my friends, enjoying the weather, or at least looking at colleges with my parents, I spent just lying across my bed, scrolling down my social media timelines, looking at what everyone else was doing.

The closest thing to fun I experienced was actually walking to the park with Tyler and watching him play ball with his friends, Billy and Craig. They didn't particularly need me there, but I had no other way to escape.

I had no desire to focus on anything about my life or what to do with myself. The only thing I was concerned about was figuring out a way to make my parents stay together.

My friend, Shelby, and I had talked about the situation a few times; but I knew she would never understand, because she hadn't lived with her parents since she was a little girl.

One thing I knew was that being without both of my parents, together, would only make my life more miserable.

One evening, after we were all home and settled for the night, my parents rents called us into the living room for a family discussion about what the plans would be before, during, and after the separation.

I knew this talk wasn't something I was looking forward to. I just knew it had to be done, so I made up my mind that I would just sit there and let them talk. I knew nothing Tyler or I said would ever make a difference.

We all sat down, and Dad turned the TV off. The only thing we heard were the crickets outside the open window as the breeze gently blew in. The tension still found a way of suffocating me. Those dreadful feelings, similar to sitting in the dentist chair, waiting to get a tooth pulled.

I felt my palms sweating and my body being overcome by nausea and anxiety. Crying would have been most appropriate; yet it wasn't such a good idea, considering I had no idea what was going to be said.

I hoped that I would hear my parent apologize for the misunderstanding and that everything about the divorce was just a ridiculous hoax to see how Tyler and I would actually react to being in limbo while our future weighed in the balance. I braced myself for the steep drop in this roller coaster of emotions I had experienced for the past few months.

"We decided the best thing for us to do was to sit down and talk about a plan for when things are finalized," Dad said.

He looked at me and Tyler, from his recliner, leaning forward, with his hands folded and his elbows digging into his knees. "No matter what we decide, I know it won't be any easier for you all than it will be for me. I want nothing more than for you guys to be happy, so I'll do my best—as I've always done—to make sure you are, even if it causes my life discomfort."

"I feel like all this happened because of me," Tyler mumbled, as he looked down at the floor.

"Why would you think some nonsense like that?" Mom said. She reached over and rubbed her hand on Tyler's head.

"If I weren't playing basketball, Dad and Nikki wouldn't feel like they had to be at every game, and you wouldn't feel so left out all of the time. We would all be at the house, together, eating dinner or doing things; together, like we used to do back in the day."

Dad stood up and looked at my mom like he really wanted to say something to her, but he focused his attention on me and Tyler, instead.

"We're separating because of us, not you two. We're the ones who made the vows to be together for better or for worse, in good times and in bad, and whatever else we said at that time," Dad said, as he threw his hand to the side.

"Maybe, if you remembered the vows you made, we wouldn't be having this discussion right now, would we?" Mom said. "That's the problem with people these days. Vows are just something people say and never mean. They never think that what they're saying is something they have to actually live by. Yes, I go to church a lot. No, I haven't been to every single game."

"Angela, when is the last time you've actually been to a game, tell me that! If you happen to show up, you're either late, not sitting with us, standing off to the side, waiting to escape, or complaining about being late for service because you came!" Dad said.

"Ricky, please!" Mom exclaimed. "You mean to tell me that you don't want to be with me anymore because I'm not obsessed with Tyler's basketball games?"

"I'm telling you that I don't think you've made ANY effort to do anything for anyone unless it was for church, on your way to church, or on your way home from church. You have made those people your entire life, instead of making your FAMILY your entire life.

"Why are we forever having this conversation? What is your issue with me and your children that you don't want to be with us? What has the Lord done for you that you completely forgot about the family he blessed you with? Do you know how many people wish they had your life?

"You have two amazing kids; and you have a husband who loves you, goes to work, pays the bills, and supports his kids. Even the Bible says if you don't provide help and support to your family, you have denied your faith and are worse than an unbeliever."

"You're talking about that verse in first Timothy, chapter five?"

"I don't know where it is. I know it's in there, though. You know what it says!"

"So you mean to tell me that there aren't men at the church who look at me and wonder why my husband doesn't support me at church, doesn't want to hear me speak, or doesn't wonder why my children don't support me when I have programs? Do you know how difficult it is when everyone knows I have a family, but they never come to anything I've spearheaded?" Mom said.

She trembled, as tears welled up in her eyes.

"Don't you dare go playing the victim. These kids should come first. There should be no question about that," Dad said.

He pointed at us, while he looked Mom in her face.

"If you took your rightful place as the head of this household…" Mom screamed.

"Really, Angela? Rightful place? It looks like you want to wear the pants in this relationship.

"And just because I don't do what you say, you make life hell for everyone. That can't be what you preach about in church. I don't know the entire Word of God, but your behavior toward this family cannot possibly reflect what I've heard.

"You're a hypocrite, preaching and teaching to those people the right way to be, while your own family is falling apart. You think the image everyone sees is flawless, don't you? I doubt it. If you knew what they really think of you—running back and forth, leaving your family multiple nights a week—you'd stop making such a clown of yourself."

Where Do We Go From Here?

My mom just sat there, huffing and puffing. Her head shook, and she closed her eyes as tight as she could. I had never seen her so frustrated in my entire life.

"Mom, Dad, may I say something, please?" Tyler asked, cautiously.

Neither of them said a word.

"I feel very uncomfortable every single time you two have a talk about this family. It always comes back to the very same thing. Dad, you don't want Mom to go to church; you want her to spend time with us. Mom, it seems like you don't want to spend time with us. Is that the case? Is it?"

"Why would you say something like that, Ty?" Mom said, with a strange tone to her voice.

"Well, it seems like you don't want to do what the rest of us are doing. I don't know why you always find a way out of doing things with the rest of us. It feels like you don't love us as much as you love the church."

"Well, that's not true. I think we all have a large part to play in all of this. It's not just me," Mom said, in a defensive tone. "We all have some changes to make. No one has really made an attempt to change anything, and we have all gone too far and stayed too long."

"What could Tyler or I have done to make sure things went differently between you and Dad? We don't control what you two do," I said.

I felt myself getting upset. My dad raised his eyebrows and looked at Mom.

She snapped. "Don't sit there and make this all about me. I'm going in my room, because this conversation is going nowhere at all. None of you want to change. None of you are thinking about what I go through in my life, knowing the way you all feel—none of you have a desire to go to church with me.

"The thought of knowing that my family could die and find themselves in Hell for eternity doesn't sit well with me, at all. I have tried to be an example by loving on you all and showing you the right way to live; yet your hang-up is with me, because I don't go to basketball games or go out to eat with you?

"You all have some serious soul-searching to do. I'm not the one who needs to get right with God. Jesus is coming, soon. I don't want Him to return and find me arguing with you all about basketball games and sitting at home with you."

"Nice, Ange. Tell us how you really feel," Dad said, as he headed toward the kitchen. "I don't have time for this mess. It never fails! As soon as you realize how wrong you are for the way things are around here, you tell us we're all going to Hell. I knew it was coming. If I'm going to Hell for wanting you to spend time with us, I guess I'll also see you there for being a charlatan."

Mom kept walking. Nothing else was said between the two of them. From the looks of things, the meeting was over.

Tyler grabbed his ball, and we went outside to take a walk.

"Okay, Nikki. What do you think is the best thing for us to do? This is crazy! I can't even believe we're actually having this conversation," Tyler said, while bouncing the ball down the sidewalk.

"Well, the fact that Mom does all the cooking and the laundry are pretty good things, right?" I said.

I didn't really feel good that I could only find two positive things about Mom.

"Yeah. She does pray for us, and all that, when we aren't feeling well and when things are coming up. That makes us feel a little better, right?"

"Yeah. That's good, but I don't feel like her praying all the time. It's annoying, sometimes, no matter how good it is for us, right?"

"Yeah. I hear you. Prayer is necessary, and Mom is gonna pray for us whether we're with her or not, isn't she?"

"Yeah. She will pray, regardless."

"Okay. So what do we love about Dad?"

"Dad comes to my games and takes us places when we need rides. He's fun, for the most part, but he's usually in his own world."

I looked at Tyler and started thinking about how things might go if we lived with Dad. I told him I thought it was better to just leave it alone, if we could. I knew when I told him, that we could not possibly leave it alone and let them decide.

Our parents have become total opposites over the years. It became clear, this was going to be an ugly divorce. Mom and Dad didn't love each other anymore, and it was clear that they didn't want to compromise, forgive, or reconcile—under any circumstances.

The divorce made me feel like someone was dying. I had never gone through anything so devastating. Tyler and I weren't the best kids in the world. Maybe we should have gotten along a little better and not caused so much stress on Mom and Dad.

I pondered if Dad was stressed out because he was always the one doing sports with us; if Mom was stressed out about other things, and if that's why she was always at church trying to get help. I really didn't know what to make of it.

One thing I was clear about was that I'm embarrassed that we were even going through it. I didn't know if they would ask me why and then start asking me all the things that I already asked Tyler.

I'm sure they would ruminate on my half-sister, Melissa, coming into the picture as the real reason. Nobody knew the entire story, just whatever had been pieced together through the gossip that circulated in church, at the beauty salon, and other places.

What we knew as normal, would never be again. There would be no more family vacations. There would be no more sitting in the kitchen looking at Dad telling corny jokes and looking at Mom as she rolled her eyes. I would never see Mom fix Dad's plate again. I would never see the two of them curled up on the couch, watching movies, together. We would probably never go out to eat again, either.

The life I took for granted was over. Jynea and Shelby never lived with their dads, so telling them what I was going through wouldn't have helped.

The next few weeks were filled with pain, frustration, and confusion. It was so hard being between Mom and Dad. Our family unit was being eaten up, like a cancer, by this extreme case of divorce. Each week seemed to have reached another level of agony and grief. We felt the weakness increasing daily. The pulse of love that kept us holding on to one another grew more and more faint, as we entered the hospice stage of our ending.

The moment Mom told me they would be seeing separate attorneys to get everything divided between the two of them, they became even more irritated with one another.

Dad didn't desire to be there. I overheard him telling his friend, Rodney, he didn't want to be around anymore, but he couldn't afford to move out because of other financial obligations.

I didn't know exactly what those obligations were. He said he would stay, until he had to leave.

I noticed he would sleep on the couch, and Mom would spend most of her time in the bedroom with the door closed. They did, however, continue to parent us together; but we didn't sit at the table for meals as a family.

I felt like being at home was more stressful than being anywhere else. As much as I hated being at work, taking orders as a cashier or bussing tables at the restaurant, it was better than having to deal with being around either of them. I started telling Kathy to schedule me every Sunday. I didn't mind working on Saturdays, either.

We weren't even on life support; we were just letting it happen. No one in our house put forth a bit of effort to reverse any of it. It was happening, and there was no way to pull it back together. It would take a miracle, seriously.

CHAPTER TWO

NO ONE UNDERSTANDS

A few weeks had passed and things were increasingly depressing. Shelby was the only one in my life who knew how to get my mind off things and to change my perspective on the worst of situations.

A few months after we learned that Shelby was pregnant, she gave birth to a beautiful baby boy, Jason Rashawn McDaniel Jr. She made up the nickname LJ (short for lil Jason).

Our relationship changed, but she didn't...we didn't give up on what we had. We knew we needed one another for the support and encouragement we didn't receive from our own immediate families.

Yes, our circumstances were different and, even as best friends, we disregarded one another's feelings, at times, with a lack of communication and empathy.

Shelby wanted to get out of the house and visit, because there weren't many places she could bring an infant. Having a baby really changed her perspective on life.

Jason Sr. was arrested, halfway through the pregnancy, for being in the wrong place at the wrong time, once again. I assumed he would start doing things much differently after the shooting, but he returned to the same riotous behavior. Jason loved to live very freely, until he was caught and contained.

How does a person maintain the ability to sit still in prison, but was unable to be still when he's home?

It was difficult to understand a lifestyle I had never experienced. My grandmother (Mom-Mom as I called her), always told me not to judge someone, if I hadn't walked a mile in their shoes. I tried not to, but I still found myself giving Jason the side eye—Shelby as well, for dealing with him.

"When I look at my baby, I want to give him all the love my parents never gave me," Shelby said, as she rocked LJ to sleep on my bed.

"I know what you mean. Do you ever doubt that you can, though? How do you think you can do that?" I said.

I wanted to believe her but wasn't sure if she even understood what she was saying.

"Look at this little boy, Nikki. Are you kidding me, right now? My baby is dope. He has three pairs of J's and a North Face, plus all these clothes with tags that his godfather bought him. He wants for nothin'."

"Well, that's all well and good. But, like right now, he sleeps in the bed with you and sometimes you run out of formula and all that."

"What's your point? I feel like you've been a little shady toward me since I got pregnant with LJ, and I don't know why. Is it your Mom that's making you look at me like a bad person?"

"No, I don't think she said anything mean about you. I know she doesn't want me to do the same thing you did, though," I said, shrugging my shoulders.

"I didn't mean to get myself in this situation. I was in love with Jason; I still love him, to this day. No matter what you—or anyone else—have to say about him, he was there for me when everyone else was worrying about themselves.

"Yes, he's locked up now, but he writes me every single week. The letters he writes to me and LJ are enough to make me feel better than when I'm with the people I see every single day. I know I'm on his mind.

"The fact that he's in there, and I know where he is and what he's doing, makes me feel better. He has started going to the Bible study in there. He's changing."

"What makes you think he's actually changing? I thought he was changing before, but he still went right back out to the streets, hustling and hanging with the guys he always got in trouble with."

"I know he's changing because of how he talks to me, now. He tells me he didn't realize how much LJ and I meant to him, until now. He tells me, all the time, how much better things are going to be when he gets home."

"Better? How will they be better? You know how hard it is to find a job when you've been in a lot of trouble?"

"How do you know? How many people do you know who got out of jail and started working?"

"I've just heard, that's all. Sorry, I don't personally know any ex-prisoners. My mom's cousin Robbie is in prison, but I don't know when he's getting out. He's been locked up for a minute. I don't know if he ever had a real job though."

"While you're sitting there, looking at me like a loser, I still have someone who loves me for me and is going to come home to me and our baby. We're going to make this work. I'm not going to be like my mom, with all these different guys in my life. I will go to school and work and take care of our son so, hopefully, we'll have a place together and live the life we both deserve."

"Okay?" I said to Shelby, with a confused look on my face.

I had no idea why she became so defensive, when I only expressed my concern for her and the baby. I honestly could not have cared less about Jason; I knew he was nothing but a liar. He always threw caution to the wind. Whatever he felt like doing, that's exactly what he would do.

It was interesting how he never realized he loved Shelby and their then unborn baby while he was running around with other females and hanging with his cousins in the streets.

Shelby was addicted to that drug we called Jason, and she didn't want an intervention. She loved being emotionally high off the words he said, even if she knew he wasn't telling the truth. He intoxicatingly fed her heart with the words she believed, and it all made sense to her. There was no way of getting her to see how poisonous he was to her life. She lived in the valley of the shadow of death.

Her father wasn't there to protect her from guys like Jason, because he was the same type of guy. Her mom, Miss Charlene, didn't teach her anything about womanhood, because she didn't know how to be a lady herself.

I figured it was best I ended the conversation.

Just then, I heard a knock on my bedroom door. It was my mom, of course.

"Come in," I said, actually relieved that my mom came to the door.

It felt really uncomfortable, having ended the conversation with Shelby about her situation.

"Hey, girls. I'm getting ready to run to the store. Shelby, do you need anything? We can run by the store, and then I will take you and 'Man-Man' home."

(This was my mom's way of getting rid of Shelby when she's exhausted her welcome.)

"Sounds good to me," Shelby said.

She sighed, while reaching with one arm to gather LJ's belongings and to toss them in her diaper bag.

We grabbed the rest of our things and went outside. Shelby secured the baby in his car seat carrier. My mom came outside a few moments later, and we all got in the car.

It was quiet, until LJ realized we weren't in the house anymore. He was the only baby I knew who did NOT like car rides. Now that I think of it, I didn't know any other babies. I just thought all babies like riding in cars, for some reason.

"Oh my God, LJ!" Shelby shouted, in utter frustration.

Her baby screamed and squirmed, as if he sat on hot coals, struggling to free himself from his seat.

"It's okay, Man-Man," Mom said, as she turned the music up.

"Where's his binky, Shelby?" I asked, hoping to show her I was concerned.

"Hmmm, well if I knew, it would be in his mouth, Nikki. I thought I put it in this side pocket when I was picking up everything off your bed."

"I didn't see it on my bed at all. I thought it was clipped on his shirt or something."

"Well, it's not. I'm just going to pick him up, Miss Angela," Shelby said, like she was going to do it whether my mom liked it or not.

"No, Shelby, we're going to be at the store in a few minutes, and I don't want to get a ticket for the baby not being in his seat. Besides that, it's just dangerous. We don't want anything to happen to him, do we?" she said, in a condescending tone.

Shelby didn't say a word, and LJ kept screaming. She put her chin in her hand and leaned on the door, as she looked out the window. That was always an issue with Shelby; she never wanted anyone to say anything to her about how she took care of her baby.

I heard some plastic rattling in the backseat where they were sitting. Shelby took an airhead out of her pocket and leaned toward the car seat. Just then, much-needed silence filled the car.

"Here you go, Fat-Fat," Shelby said.

She chuckled at LJ, eating the candy.

"Mommy is going to get you quiet, one way or the other, even if it hurts your little tummy, isn't she, Man?" my mom said, as she turned onto the highway.

This was her way of talking to Shelby but acting like she was talking to the baby.

No one said a word. A few minutes later, we arrived at Target and pulled into a parking space next to where customers (should) put carts after shopping. I jumped out, grabbed a cart, and pulled it next to the car, so Shelby could sit the car seat in it.

Once we all walked in the store, Mom took the cart and LJ and told us she would meet us at the front of the store in fifteen minutes.

"If I knew she was gonna take him with her, I woulda stayed in the car," Shelby said, jokingly.

"Shut up. He's a good baby, as long as he gets his way," I said to Shelby.

I pushed her shoulder, like I wanted to beat her up.

We walked down the aisle, and Shelby grabbed a box of cereal and some noodles, to eat for later, I suppose. I really didn't want to ask any questions. I know that she had her own way of surviving in the situation she was in, and I wanted to make sure that she didn't feel like I was judging her.

After picking up a few more items, we found our way to the front of the store, where my mom was with LJ and a cart full of baby items. It looked like Christmas for Shelby.

One thing I could say about my mom was that she was very in tune with doing for others when she saw a need. I never quite understood how she saw others' needs but never the needs of anyone in our household.

I was happy for Shelby, for the moment. I knew she needed things for her baby. She was always too prideful to ask, or maybe she really couldn't deal with the rejection of someone telling her no as much as Miss Charlene did.

"Wow! What's all this stuff, Miss Angela? Is this for us?" Shelby said, looking through the bottles, diapers, clothes, and wipes in the cart.

"Yes, this is all for the baby. I didn't make it to your shower, but I wanted to make sure LJ had everything he needs. I figured the things I bought were items he could use at some point. I hope you don't mind."

"No, I don't mind. Thank you so much, but is it okay if we get Huggies instead of the store brand? I like for my baby to have the best, and I don't want him to have any leaks. I don't like the way these wipes smell that you chose, either. Can I switch those out for something else? The cucumber scented ones are so much better."

I looked at my mom, and she looked like she wanted to say something; but surprisingly enough, she didn't. She peacefully looked at Shelby, and I knew it was coming at a later time. I honestly believed my mom had a lot to say. She always hated how people who had the least, seemingly complained about everything they were given, as if they could possibly do better for themselves.

After Shelby replaced everything in the cart with the items she believed were more satisfactory for LJ, we went to the checkout line and then headed back to the car.

On the ride home, the baby nodded off, like a little old man, and we welcomed the peace and quiet with open arms.

"Thanks again for all that stuff, Miss Angela."

"I'm glad I'm blessed to be a blessing. I know how difficult it can be to take care of an infant. I had a husband, and it was difficult; so, I can only imagine what you're going through. How have you adjusted to everything since he's been born, anyway?"

"It's been hard, since it's just me and the baby most of the time. I was so tired the first month. My mom told me that she wasn't going to help me, because it would make it easier for me to go out and get pregnant all over again.

"She asks me how I am, and how LJ is, sometimes; but she never asks about Jason, even though she knows I love him and want to be with him when he gets home."

"Well, my advice to you is just focus on being the best you there is for this beautiful little baby. All he has is you. Don't worry about what anyone else is, and isn't, doing. Look to the Lord to provide for the two of you. I decree and declare that He will!"

"Thanks."

"I know you kids don't want to hear all of that, but that's all I can tell you. I have gone through so much throughout the years, and I've watched God continue to shower my family with blessings and protection, during the most difficult times. I really appreciate all He has done for us, and I owe it all to Him."

"Okay."

Awkward silence filled the car. The only thing we heard was the road noise as we headed back up the highway going home.

After a few minutes, we reached the development where Shelby lived. As soon as Mom put the car in park, the doors automatically unlocked and she popped the trunk.

I saw Miss Charlene's car in her designated parking space, so I decided to help Shelby bring her things to the door. She grabbed the car seat, the diaper bag, and one of the shopping bags. I got out of the car, determined to make only one trip to the front door of the apartment.

"Thanks again. I'll see y'all, later."

"You're welcome, Shel. Please tell your mom I said hello."

I grabbed everything from the trunk, brought it to the door for Shelby, gave her a big hug, and ran back to the car.

"That was fun, wasn't it?" Mom said, while driving.

"Yeah, fun. How cute is LJ?"

"Cute enough to keep me from ever wanting to see you experience what Shelby is going through, that's for sure."

"Well, the fact that I'm still a virgin would make me a few steps away from being in her shoes. I don't think I'm ready for any of that now, anyway."

"No, you're not ready for ANY of it. The emotional and the physical responsibility is a lot to deal with. I don't think you would like it at all. It's actually very exhausting."

"Is that why you're always at church? Because your home life is so exhausting?"

"Is that what you think? You all wear me down so badly, that I have to go to church to get away from you?"

"I don't know, maybe."

"I go to church because I know God has called me to teach the Gospel and reach those who are lost. I have always felt this way; but I was running from my calling, since I didn't feel I was worthy of carrying such a huge responsibility.

"I wanted to do it, but not at the expense of leaving behind my own fleshly desires. I felt like I needed to be somewhere I was appreciated, and where people complimented my efforts. When I'm at church, people notice me. They acknowledge me, and it feels good. I absolutely love it. This is how I know that I am meant to do what I'm doing, in ministry."

"Alrighty then."

"What is that supposed to mean?"

"Nothing. Sorry you don't feel appreciated at home by me, Dad, and Tyler. I feel pretty bad now. It's almost like we ran you off, to church, and that's why you're never around."

"It's not just that, Nikki. I really know there's a work to be done, and I want to do what God called me to do, which is to help others get to know Him."

"Did you ever try to get Dad to get to know who God is?"

"Of course, but your father isn't at a place where his heart has softened enough for me to witness to him. God told me to just keep loving your father. When the time comes, He will transform our family."

"It looks like our family is going through a transformation now, isn't it? Like falling completely apart. It's crumbling right before our eyes, like a natural disaster."

"Yes, I agree it seems that way. Yet, I know what God told me, and I have no other choice but to trust Him. I have absolutely nothing to lose."

way; but I was running from my calling, since I didn't feel I was worthy of carrying such a huge responsibility.

"I wanted to do it, but not at the expense of leaving behind my own fleshly desires. I felt like I needed to be somewhere I was appreciated, and where people complimented my efforts. When I'm at church, people notice me. They acknowledge me, and it feels good. I absolutely love it. This is how I know that I am meant to do what I'm doing, in ministry."

"Alrighty then."

"What is that supposed to mean?"

"Nothing. Sorry you don't feel appreciated at home by me, Dad, and Tyler. I feel pretty bad now. It's almost like we ran you off, to church, and that's why you're never around."

"It's not just that, Nikki. I really know there's a work to be done, and I want to do what God called me to do, which is to help others get to know Him."

"Did you ever try to get Dad to get to know who God is?"

"Of course, but your father isn't at a place where his heart has softened enough for me to witness to him. God told me to just keep loving your father. When the time comes, He will transform our family."

"It looks like our family is going through a transformation now, isn't it? Like falling completely apart. It's crumbling right before our eyes, like a natural disaster."

"Yes, I agree it seems that way. Yet, I know what God told me, and I have no other choice but to trust Him. I have absolutely nothing to lose."

CHAPTER THREE

CONTINUED FRUSTRATION

Although we had been going through our share of daily frustration, I noticed Mom had become a little more conscious of the amount of time she spent with us. She knew how hurt Tyler was from the emotional pain he displayed, from day to day. It was very difficult seeing his long face. Nothing seemed to comfort him.

Mom cooked his favorite meal: fried chicken, white rice with lots of butter, and French cut string beans. The house smelled like heaven; Tyler's face still looked like he was in Hell.

"When's your next game, Ty?" Mom asked, while fixing his plate.

"Thursday is your church night," he scoffed.

"Well, I was thinking I would take you to the game and stay for the whole thing. What do you think about that?"

"Really?"

"Yes, really!"

Just then, Dad walked in the front door, and Tyler's face lit up. I don't think any of us had seen him smile for weeks.

"Hey, Dad. Mom is coming to my game on Thursday. She said she's going to drive me there and stay for the entire thing, even though it's her church night."

"You mean to tell me, after all this time, all I had to do was file for divorce to get Angie to show up for a game? Humph! Who knew?!"

"Please, Rick. Don't start. Here I am, trying to make things right for my children, yet you still have something smart to say. I'm not trying to win with you anymore. I'm trying to win with them."

"I sure wish someone wanted to win with me, that's for sure."

"I have tried, over and over, to win with you. I'm sorry if what I was doing wasn't good enough for you. I didn't make a conscious effort to fail you."

"Yeah, yeah, yeah, I know. You were the perfect wife, with the ungrateful husband. Here we go, again."

"I'm going in the kitchen to clean up. I've had the worst headache all day, and arguing with you certainly isn't making it any better."

"I'll come help you, Mom," I said, following her into the kitchen.

Tyler went in his bedroom, clearly upset that his good news was derailed by another petty argument between our parents. He couldn't catch a break. His bout of excitement and much-needed positivity lasted an entire two minutes before it evaporated into thin air.

Immediately after walking into the kitchen, my mom sat on a chair at the table. She said she didn't feel right. She started squinting and, suddenly, the right side of her face slid down, like a melting candle.

"Mom? What's wrong with your face?"

"Huh?"

"Mom! Mom!" I said, as I rushed to her. She started tilting over. "Dad! Ty! Help, help! Something's wrong with Mom. Hurry!"

My father ran into the kitchen and helped me lift my mother off the chair. I didn't let her hit the floor, but her dead weight was too much for me to support on my own. I looked into my mom's eyes and saw nothing but horror. Tyler's face was blank, and his mouth was open as he stood stiff, with nothing but sheer confusion and shock.

Time seemed to tick slowly, as if we were seeing everything in slow motion. My heart was pounding, and I couldn't seem to grasp exactly what was happening.

"Call 9-1-1," Dad said. "You know what? Forget it. Help me get her in the truck. I'm not sitting here, waiting on them. I don't wanna take that chance."

"But... Dad, what if...?"

"Didn't I just say help me get her in the car?"

"Yes."

"Well, do it! I don't need your advice."

Tyler and my Dad carried Mom to the Tahoe, while I held the door open. I heard my dad calling one of his friends, to get a police escort to the hospital, only three miles away.

"Can we come with you?" I asked, shaking uncontrollably.

"No, baby girl. I promise, I will call you as soon as I know what's going on. I promise," Dad said.

He hopped in the driver's side of the truck and closed the door.

Just like clockwork, we heard sirens from his friend's patrol car, coming down the street. The car stopped at the curb. As soon as my dad backed out of the driveway, they both zoomed toward St. Peter's Hospital.

I looked at Tyler, as tears rolled down his face. We both stood in the driveway and held each other, unsure if we would ever see our mother again. It became very evident in that moment that life would NEVER BE THE SAME AGAIN.

CHAPTER FOUR

THE WORDS OF A MOTHER

The church was our family. We did Easter programs in the spring, cookouts and vacation Bible school in the summer, Christmas programs and other holidays in the winter, together. There were very few things we did that our church family wasn't there for us.

We supported one another at sporting events (with the exception of football on Sundays) and graduations, birthday parties, funerals, and anything else that we considered major life events.

I recalled going to church with my mom and sister, every Sunday, while my dad stayed home to do housework or just relax. He read the Sunday paper at the kitchen table, while we got ready for church.

He didn't seem to be very angry that we were going. As a matter of fact, he never said a word about it at all. The one thing I knew was that when we talked about church, he would maintain a positive demeanor. He smiled when I shared my Sunday school lessons with him.

From the time I was a little girl, I have never remembered a time that God didn't play a large part in my life. My mother and aunt had always told my sister and me how important it was to have a relationship with God.

We were always in church. It was something that we did because my mom always made us feel like life wouldn't work out right if we didn't go. I can honestly say, I was afraid—at times—not to do right, because I believed something terrible would happen if I went astray.

There was a girl, Tracy, I knew from high school, who used to sneak out and go to parties at night, when her parents were sleeping. I recalled one time she had gone out, gotten drunk, and didn't remember what happened the night before. It was said that she woke up in a stranger's bed and when her parents found out what happened, her life was never the same.

How her life changed, no one ever detailed. She may have been someone they used as a way to scare us from sneaking out.

One day, my father and I were having a conversation about life. I believed in my heart that it was a good idea to question him about why he never wanted to come to church. I believed that he knew my need to know would come, eventually. So, it was almost like he was prepared for it.

"Dad, may I ask you something, without you becoming upset with me?" I asked, while he watched The Honeymooners.

"Absolutely. What is it, sweetheart?"

"Well, I just wonder why you never come to church with us. I know that you're home when we leave on Sunday mornings, and you're usually here when we get home. Why don't we go, together, as a family?"

"I don't really believe in going to a place where poorly educated Pentecostal preachers are telling me what 'God said'. Why is it that they know so much about what God said, but no one can answer simple questions?"

"Simple questions like what, Dad?" I said, very concerned.

"Well, for one, if there really is a God, why are there starving people in the world? Why would God have children born into such terrible situations, starving and diseased?" Dad said.

He looked at me, waiting for an answer.

"I don't know why it is the way it is."

"Well, why do people walk around hurting and killing one another, for no reason, just because they feel like it?"

"I don't know, Dad. I was kinda talking about you. I was wondering why you don't go to church."

"Well, Angel, I don't go to church because I don't believe that it's a place for me. I don't want to praise a God that would allow these things to happen to other people, while I sit here with a happy life. I don't know what it would take to make me want to go.

"The preachers, who whoop and holler and sweat and stomp while they preach, are just too much for me. I don't need the theatrics. When I try to have a discussion with them about the same questions I asked you just now, they get upset with me. The truth is, they don't have the answers I'm looking for, so I would rather leave it alone and rest on Sunday, without feeling like I have to be anywhere or do anything."

As time went on, I started to understand my dad's view on religion and church, so I decided that I would just leave it alone. I didn't want my personal faith to waver, especially since I believed everything my mother told me about God. It wasn't so much that I had personally experienced God in my adolescent years, I just trusted that what my mother said was true.

Why would my mother encourage her children to do something that wasn't beneficial to their lives?

Deep down inside, no matter what anyone said, I knew God was real. There were so many scriptures that made so much sense to me. The Word of God was always full of wisdom to guide us through life and to help keep life simple.

CHAPTER FIVE

NO GOING BACK

During my teen years, I believe, the more I was exposed to the world around me, the harder it became to have my own solid relationship with God. It was during this time I realized the relationship I had with God was not a personal one; it was, more or less, a relationship I had with God, by way of my mother.

I believed in God and knew that He was real. I even believed there was a Heaven and a Hell. The one thing I could see was that I came to realize what the flesh was, and how much of a strong hold it had on me and the people around me.

By the time I was fourteen, I had seen a few movies and heard a few songs while hanging out with my older cousins at my Aunt Ethel's house. There were some things in that house that my mom didn't completely agree with, but Aunt Ethel was my dad's sister, and he wanted me to have a relationship with my cousins.

I specifically remembered one weekend I stayed the night. My cousin, Kammy, and I was watching a rated R movie, which were not allowed in my parents' home. I sat there, completely fascinated by what I saw. I had never seen nor experienced that level of intimacy before, and I knew that Kammy noticed it.

"You never saw a love scene before?" Kammy asked me, with a smirk on her face.

"Not really. We don't have these channels at home," I stuttered.

"It's no big deal really, but I wouldn't run home and tell your parents that you saw this here. They may not let you come back."

"I'm not a baby. Why would I tell?" I asked, trying to prove to Kammy that I was mature enough to keep a secret.

"Just go in the room with Robbie," Kammy said.

She shoved me out of her bedroom, into the hall, and slammed the door.

As I walked down the hall toward Robbie's room, I heard the bass thumping from the music he was listening to. The sounds were very deep, very groovy. I couldn't quite understand all the lyrics, but Robbie seemed to be shouting them, word for word.

This music didn't sound like anything I had ever heard in my parents' house. All my mother really listened to was the Winans, the Williams Brothers, the Clark Sisters, and Shirley Caesar. My father enjoyed listening to Otis Redding, Gladys Knight and the Pips, the Dells, and whatever smooth jazz musicians that came on the radio.

"Uh, yeah, yeah!" Robbie said.

Rocking and pointing at his stereo, he listened to his song.

I stood at the doorway of his bedroom, as he sat on the edge of his bed, seemingly in another world, enjoying the music.

"What are you looking at? You never heard this song before?" Robbie asked.

He turned to me with a confused look on his face.

"No. Who is that?" I said.

I had a disgusted look on my face, as I became defensive and guarded my ignorance.

"Oh wow, this is Slick Rick!"

He laughed, as if everyone on earth should know who this man with that accent was.

I just stood there with my arms folded.

"Okay, so do you know who Big Daddy Kane is?"

"Ummm, no."

"Tribe Called Quest?"

"Uh, uh."

"Are you kidding me?" Robbie said, as he stomped his foot on the floor. "Your parents must have you living under a rock! Why don't you watch music videos when you get home from school, before they get home from work?"

"My dad is home when I get home from school. He tells Tyler and me that we have to do our homework and do our chores before we can turn the TV on during the week. By the time we actually turn the TV on, we have to watch shows together—if we aren't going to church with our mother in the evening."

"Wow, you're really living the life," Robbie said, sarcastically, as he patted my back and shook his head. "I'm going to make a tape for you to listen to when you get home. It's going to have what the rest of the world is listening to while you're at home being sheltered. You have to learn this music. It's part of who we are."

From that point forward, I learned that I had to look at the world around me and see it for what it was. This world was so full of experiences and lessons to learn, and I knew nothing besides what happened in school and in church.

I knew my parents were trying to protect me, but the way they went about it was so extreme. I knew at some point, with the help of some very resourceful people in my life, I would find my way. I was determined.

CHAPTER SIX

REAL LOVE

Going into my young adult years were very difficult. The way that I believed was the way I wanted to go, it actually became the most turbulent period of my life, altogether.

I met Rick in college, and I believed that he would help me get exactly what I wanted out of life. I looked to him to listen to me when I was most stressed out.

The relationship with my parents was so strained; they were still trying to control me, from a distance. I never liked how much they warned me about college life and how dangerous things were on campus, although neither of them had ever experienced it.

Rick and I studied together, went to parties, and enjoyed spending time with our friends as much as we could. We actually leaned on each other. I started to feel like the relationship with God that I had was not something that I needed as much as my mother tried to get me to believe.

I felt so free, not going to church all week long and not being made to feel so horrible about wanting to just relax and listen to whatever music I wanted to. I liked the different moods I experienced from listening to R&B music. Mary J. Blige always sang those songs I could relate to. I felt like she knew exactly what life was about. Her music spoke directly to me.

I remembered weeks and months would pass, and I wouldn't even bother praying. It wasn't even something that I felt like I needed to do anymore. My mindset became whatever I wanted, I would just make happen. I didn't really need to pray to make it happen. I would do whatever it was in my life that made me happy.

I had lived so much of my life doing what my parents told me to do.

"You don't need to go to that party. You don't need a boyfriend," they had said.

So many of my decisions were made for me, by them, that I never really felt like I knew what it was I liked, until they told me.

My college major, Business Management, was chosen by my dad. I didn't even want to go to college. He told me if I ever wanted to be successful in life, I would have to go to college.

I was so irritated by what he and my mother said about college; the two of them never went to college, and we were living a very comfortable life. We didn't live in a fancy house or in an expensive neighborhood, but where we lived was very comfortable. I never really wanted much. I just wanted to have a happy family who traveled and lived a balanced life—something that my parents never did.

After I graduated college, Rick told me he wanted to settle down and get married. I knew marriage was something that I wanted. I hadn't really been the most outgoing person I wanted to be. I never felt confident enough to be part of the biggest cliques and hang with the most popular people. I just wanted to move forward in life and raise a family with the love of my life. And that was exactly what we did.

Ricky and I got married and decided that we would live life on our own terms. It wouldn't be what my parents wanted, and he wouldn't live the rest of his life being angry or annoyed about the way things went when he was younger. The support we needed, we would give to one another. No one else mattered. This was our life, our marriage, and we would control what we wanted and how well we did in life.

CHAPTER SEVEN

CHANGES

The first few years of marriage were challenging. I knew that it would be. This was the first time that I had ever actually lived with another man besides my father.

Since my dad was a military man, he was a very neat and on-time individual. There were very few times I went in my dad's closet and observed any of his personal items out of order. When I looked on his dresser in the bedroom, everything had its place. I recalled the Old Spice aftershave, the deodorant, keys, glasses, and all of his grooming tools were always in place.

Ricky was nothing like that, at all. I know he was raised in a house where his dad went to church and his mother had a drinking problem, so being neat and keeping the house clean may not have been a very big deal. I never dreamed that his messy ways would irritate me as much as they did. He would go in the kitchen after I cooked dinner, use a plate and a glass, and only wash the items he used. He would never wash all the dishes, even if I was the one who cooked.

Who does that?

I realized after about a year that we needed someone to talk to. I called my godmother and asked if she could help me sort through some of the many issues Rick and I faced with our marriage. It was very clear to me that we needed help.

I felt that he completely forgot how we were supposed to support one another as much as we had promised on our wedding day.

What happened to the idea of not needing anyone else to help us figure this out?

I just wanted to be happy again. I wanted to be in love, like we were in college, when he thought I was perfect for him.

The children came along a few years later. I started to realize we had something else to focus on besides arguing about dishes in the sink and dirty clothes on the floor. Now we had dirty diapers and bottles to deal with.

The two most absolutely amazing people in the world were the fruit of my womb. Life couldn't have been more amazing for the two of us. We knew that our goals were to be a well-rounded family, to take our children everywhere, and to teach them everything, so they will become the most confident people on earth.

Ten years into our marriage, we had two children and I felt as if I was just going through the motions. I planned so many vacations and day trips, cooked so many meals, ironed so many clothes, and went to so many parent–teacher conferences with Rick; yet, I still felt empty.

I knew he loved me, and I knew that he wanted our children happy. I felt lost and bored with life. I called my mother, and the only thing she told me was, "You have to keep praying, Ange. If you aren't praying, you need to start."

The advice my mother gave was something I knew was coming, but I just didn't want to deal with it. I just wanted to have another set of options. I wanted to do something different, for once.

Deep down inside, I knew there was a feeling of validation that I had when I was in church and everyone encouraged me for my participation. I loved to hear my pastor tell me how much God loved me and how everything would be okay, if I just kept the faith.

No matter how much I knew these things, it wasn't the same when I was home, alone, dealing with Rick and the kids.

One Friday night, my co-worker, Dora, invited me to her church for a revival. I decided to go, since I was told that the pastor who was coming always encouraged the people. He never had people standing in $100 lines, manipulating people into giving their last just to get a word from him.

Dora wasn't the average emotional Christian who let her feelings drive her decisions in life. She was a person I really trusted. I believed if she said this preacher was good, then I would go there and know that what I learned was very meaningful and helpful.

That night, I had the time of my life. I felt as though no one was in that church with me, besides the preacher and God. I felt as though everything that I was going through was being discussed across that pulpit.

The load that was lifted after crying out to God and freeing myself of all the guilt and shame of my years being a backslider was such a relief. I made a vow to God that I wouldn't let anyone or anything get in the way of our relationship, anymore.

I wanted to make sure that God had my complete attention, at all times. I don't know if I was so emotionally drained from all that had been happening over the past few years, or if I was so excited about being in that place of comfort that I had known all my life.

From that night on, I re-dedicated my life to Christ. I knew my life depended on it. There was no better decision that I could have made for myself, nor for my family. I believed that if I was in a right place, spiritually, they would be, too.

I knew this renewed journey I was on would cost me some things, including time and a few relationships with friends and family from my backsliding years. Making those changes weren't easy at all, but I felt that it was for the best.

Going to Bible study and midweek services took me away from Tyler's basketball games and watching shows at home with Ricky, but I needed to do things for me. I didn't want to lose myself in my family, once again, and allow anyone—or anything—to come between my Savior and me.

When I was in prayer and reading my Bible, meditating and listening to my music, I got through the days at work and actually enjoyed my forty-minute commute home. I took my time, relaxed on the train, looked out the window, and was at peace thinking about how blessed I was.

Nothing else was better for me than what I knew to be the safest place in the world, in the Will of God.

The more I got involved in going to church, the more my family seemed to pull at me and complain about the things I was doing. I invited Rick to church, and he said he wasn't interested. I brought the children to church with me on Sundays, and he said that he wouldn't even do that with us, as a family.

Rick told me that he would not get involved with anything that I decided to do without him. He said that church wasn't a family activity; it was something I was forcing the entire family to do.

The children and I continued to go to church. It seemed that Nikki enjoyed herself, while Tyler didn't want to be involved. The only thing he wanted to do was stay at home with his dad and play ball on Sundays.

It was a constant fight that we continued to have, until I gave up. I realized there were some fights that weren't worth having, after a certain point. I let Tyler stay with his dad, and I continued to bring Nikki with me to church. While I felt that my family was split, I wanted to be grateful that at least two of us were going.

Looking back, I believe I made the best decision for myself and my family by going back to church and having a relationship with God. The fact that my husband wanted me to choose was a matter of how he felt about church versus how he felt about me.

If he separated the two and understood that God wanted him, and not so much the church, I believe he would be a much happier person. We could still be a thriving loving family and make time for God.

If Rick wanted me to choose between my God and him, I had to make my decision and move forward. I believed with all my heart that God would honor that.

Nothing would hinder my growth. I had lost over ten years of my life, thinking I could do it all without Him. I finally came to my senses.

As time went on, I noticed myself becoming more and more distant from the things of this world. I wanted to be so close to God that I decided to find a church that would give me that feeling of family and warmth I had in church growing up.

I was going through the growing pains of marriage and realized I was in a situation I never wanted repeated from my childhood. My children and I left my husband at home, while he found more important things to do.

The man that I fell in love with, married, and had two children with became so annoyed at the fact that I wanted to be with my church family. He seemed to be as disgusted with me as he was with the church.

Whenever I told him there was a revival at church or an anniversary for the church or the pastor, his favorite line to me was, "Mo' money, Mo' money!" Rick never seemed to grasp the idea of giving unto the Lord. He wanted me to keep my money in my purse, for when I actually needed it.

Being married to Rick became more and more depressing. I don't know if it was because he was turned off from going to church, or because I was so turned off from him not coming to church with me.

Some people asked, "Why couldn't you all just enjoy this part of your life without each other and enjoy the rest of your life together?"

If I had a dollar for every moment that I tried to look passed his absence, I'd be a millionaire. There was no getting through to him to spend time with me once I returned home from church. He would sit, like a zombie, with his eyes glued to the television, ignoring and seemingly punishing me, just for wanting to be in church.

I remember talking to one of the ministers at the church, Minister Barbara.

Her words to me were, "Don't back down from the devil. He will have to come under submission, sooner or later. Keep coming to church when the doors are opened and watch God show you something you never thought you would see in your family."

Minister Barbara was right. My life evolved into a tug of war. The stress that I was under, painting this perfect picture and showing everyone how beautiful my life was, smothered me every day.

I invited my family over and Rick invited his friends and their families over for the holidays. We had the best parties. Everyone was under the impression that we had the best life. We wanted it so badly that we pretended. It felt so good to have those feelings, even if it only lasted for those few hours.

By the time Tyler and Nikki started playing sports, my home life was completely drowned in church responsibilities and my marriage was touch and go. Rick and I had agreed, years prior to my returning to church, that if we were to ever have children, we would never let anything come between us raising our children in the same house.

We wanted them to see us both regularly and to enjoy the balance of having a mother and a father in the house. We never denied how important it was for the children to see us together, as a team, handling separate responsibilities in the house.

With all of those things in mind, we never considered how important it was for us to display a happy wholesome family life. Yes, we both worked and maintained the household as a team. Yes, we slept in the same bed and occasionally went out to eat as a family. Yes, I cooked, fixed Rick's plate, and left it in the microwave for him if he worked late. But there was a great wall of division, and it was completely noticeable. The children saw it, but we were so busy doing ourselves that we forgot where this left them—emotionally broken.

I kept pressing my way to church, encouraging as many people as I could along the way, and living a victorious life. I was appreciated everywhere. People were impressed with me. My life was amazing everywhere, except at home.

The people at work knew I was a Christian. The people at the church knew I had been on my job since graduating college. They saw my children and thought I was an amazing mother. It was even encouraging some of the women that I just kept coming, knowing that my husband wanted nothing to do with the church.

They admired my bravery and steadfast strength. They said they knew I loved God and loved my husband. The picture I painted everywhere I went was beautiful! The one thing I realized was, the person I really wanted to be impressed with me, Rick, was not impressed at all.

He didn't care how much money I raised for the pastor's anniversary; he didn't care how well I did each quarter at work. He just wanted me home with him and the kids, whether he affirmed me or not. He just wanted me to be okay with myself.

CHAPTER EIGHT

GROWING PAINS

After my newly discovered stepdaughter, Melissa, came into the picture, I stopped caring about my marriage or anything that had to do with Ricky. In a way, I was grateful that I didn't have the feelings for him that would have caused me to go ape crazy on him.

The part I wasn't prepared for was the gossip that came from church members. The word traveled fast, as anyone else's information would, but strangely I didn't believe it would be the same in my case.

The people at church treated me as if my husband conceived his much older daughter during our marriage. I found myself becoming stressed about my home life at church. Church was my happy place, the place where I felt free and no one knew anything about my life.

They knew only what I let them see. They were separated from my life just the way I had meticulously planned from the very beginning. I felt my loss of control over my perfect three sliced pie of life. Everything seemed to be merging and overlapping. The insecurities I prided myself in burying surfaced.

Each day, after Melissa came into our lives, I had to try even harder to force the marriage to look like we were in a beautiful place. It ate me up inside that I couldn't express to anyone how I felt about it all.

My sister, Alice, told me that she was surprised I wasn't more hurt by it all. She was concerned that I was in denial. I assured her that I was fine and that I would be as supportive as I could, making sure Rick built a strong relationship with Melissa, as well as one with Tyler and Nikki.

The brokenness I felt with my life was the same hurt I felt all over for ten years prior. The love that I once had for God and going to church was gone. My feelings of inadequacy resurfaced, and I didn't know what more I could do to get back to my center of peace and tranquility.

I lost my sense of who I was pretending to be. That woman became a fog. Depression and anxiety made its way into my life, and the suffocating feelings of oppression rested on me and trapped me, like a leather jacket about three sizes too small. I had no idea how to make it go away.

It was at this point in my life that I realized, after all this time being in the church, going to church, raising money, leading praise and worship, making phone calls on behalf of the church, participating with the food pantry, and reading church announcements that I still didn't have a relationship with God.

What's worse, I didn't have a relationship with my husband, my children, or myself. I was putting on a show for everyone and this scene was about to end.

CHAPTER NINE

LIFE AS THE HUSBAND SEES IT

Where did I go wrong?

I had been doing all I knew to do from the very beginning of our marriage, to ensure that my wife and children had everything they needed. There was never a time when my wife needed money to get her hair done, or to buy herself anything, that I didn't give it to her.

I never knew the day would come when she felt like throwing in the towel on our relationship. We faced many obstacles, the two of us, never needing anyone to give us anything to keep our picture-perfect lives intact.

We had fun and always handled business together. I always loved being a good husband and being supportive of everything we did together. I never doubted whether she would be with me until we were parted by death.

The journey we made thus far was one that many people couldn't say they had successfully made. Our journey was well planned, as far as I was concerned. The love was there, our trust was never in question, and we depended on one another for support.

I came from parents who weren't able to provide for me the way I needed. My mother, though she loved me (I believe), had a serious alcohol problem. I was her only child, and because of that, it left me doing things for myself—and for her—that weren't generally done by a child.

Many days I came home from school, and there were empty beer cans on the coffee table and the sink was full of dirty dishes that had been in there for so many days that the entire place smelled horrible.

My father, on the other hand, was a deacon in church. He was also part of the men's ministry and the men's choir. He went to church several nights a week and lost himself in all the things he felt would help bring his spirits up.

When he was at church, nothing that happened at home was a concern for him. No one from church ever came to our home (for lack of a better term) to visit us. I'm not even sure if anyone knew why my mom seldom went to church. The reason he gave when people asked why she wasn't there was usually, "She's not feeling well today."

There were times, though, that she actually showed up. The other women at church seemed to look at her with the side eye, wondering exactly what it was that my dad actually saw in her.

My mother was a very thin woman. Her hair was pulled back in a messy French roll, which she did the night before—by piling gel on one side and poking as many hairpins as she could on the other side to hold the style together. She generally wore a short black skirt, with whatever blouse she wanted to wear that day. Her shoes were high heels, and she wore lipstick and lots of gold jewelry. I never saw her wear makeup or jewelry during the week; but when Sunday approached, very few pieces were left in her jewelry box.

Every time we went to church, it was basically the same order of service. We went in for Sunday school at 9:00 a.m.; it was finished at 10:00 a.m. After Sunday school, each class reviewed what they learned from the books that they all shared.

Once that was done, we prayed, read scripture, and then a few minutes of what they called devotional service where people stood up and testified about things God did for them throughout the week.

These testimonies were generally shared by someone who endured a difficult situation, like an unpaid bill, a sick family member, or an employment issue. By the time each testimony was over, people were excited about the story and praised God for what He did in someone else's life.

Once everyone was all wound up and excited by the testimonies, there was a selection by the choir. The choir that sang depended on which Sunday of the month it was. The men's choir sang on the first and third Sundays. The youth choir sang on the second and fourth Sundays. And the combined choirs sang together on the fifth Sundays.

Of course, the offering used to be after the choir sang, until my dad and the other deacons noticed that people purposely came to church late to avoid giving their tithes and offerings.

(That wasn't information that was directly shared with me. I overheard my parents discussing it one night when they thought I was sleeping. My mom didn't agree with it; but she wasn't on the deacon board, so her opinion didn't really matter.)

I never had a real relationship with God. I always looked at church as a place where people were manipulated into doing things that they wouldn't think to do on their own. I looked around at how the pastors preached and the people jumped up, screaming and dancing, and I wondered why I never felt anything but pure frustration.

I felt like my dad was a fraud. He went to church all week long, after working a full-time job as an accountant in the city; but he never looked to see what his family actually needed. Granted, it was only the three of us, since his parents were deceased and my mom's family lived in Texas—so we never saw them.

How could a man love the Lord so much but not love his own wife and son?

My mom worked before I was born, but I was told she fell into a deep depression shortly thereafter. She didn't seem to care about much, and my dad went through the motions to make everyone think we were doing great.

I didn't have the happiest childhood; nothing ever felt real. Everything was about my dad making everyone think we had it all together, when that was the farthest from the truth. I just went along with it, because whatever I wanted, he bought. I never witnessed a display of love and affection between my parents. I didn't think they hated one another, but it seemed like they only showed love on special occasions.

By the time I reached high school, I drowned myself in my books and sports. My goal was to get out of that apartment, go to college on a scholarship of some sort, and obtain a business degree.

There were teachers I had in my path who I talked to, and they gave me all the information I needed to get on the right track. Everyone looked at me as the guy who had it all, not knowing how much I actually lacked.

The girls in school were nice to me, very nice actually. I didn't have to work hard in school; they helped me get all my assignments done. I felt the love from everyone, except at home.

My friends and teachers made me feel like they actually liked having me around. There was never a day I went to school and felt ignored. I played basketball, and everyone cheered me on. Of all the cheers I heard, game after game, I never heard my parents cheer for me. No matter how many points, steals, or assists I made, they never knew—and they never cared enough to ask. They were doing their own things.

I never realized, until much later down the road, that their encouragement and affirmation was needed at that time more than ever. I didn't even feel like anyone cared about me or who I was, if they couldn't tell me how amazing I was with my schoolwork or on the basketball court.

In my eyes, the love I wanted was exactly what I received from those girls.

CHAPTER TEN

HIS EGO AND HIS HEART

With all the cheering and attention I received at school, I still knew something was missing.

A lot of my time was spent reading a lot of different books and trying to learn my history as an African American. We all got the typical history lessons about who Martin Luther King Jr., Marcus Garvey, and Rosa Parks were. Yes, we knew slaves came from Africa and that Harriet Tubman helped many of them escape to freedom. No one really taught me everything I wanted to know.

My parents witnessed the racial divide present when they were growing up, but no one ever really talked with me about it. I was a young Black man in America, and no one really said much to me about what to think or what could happen if I was in the wrong place at the wrong time. I was always learning things from my teachers and my friends' parents.

Many times Mr. Martin, my history teacher, challenged me to sit down and read books about something I didn't learn in school. He told me there were so many things that couldn't be covered in the school textbooks, so they taught us only bits and pieces of what they thought we needed to know about

American history. I didn't know exactly what he meant, until I started looking for more information.

One day, while I was in the public library with a list of books Mr. Martin had given me to read, I checked out a book called In Their Own Interests by Earl Lewis. This book made me look at myself, and the people around me, much differently.

I wondered what it was that drove us to be the way we were as a people. I looked at my mother, on one hand, and wondered what it was that made her the way she was. I also looked at my dad and wondered why he prided himself so much in what everyone thought of him.

The more I thought about it, the more I realized how much I was like my dad. I really didn't have a sense of who I was, though I wanted to. I wanted to make sure that every time someone saw me, I looked my best, and my hair was cut.

My mother often told me how handsome I was, so I knew she really believed it. That was probably the only compliment she gave me on a regular basis. I believed that everything I wanted I could get as long as I looked good and used my charm. I was the smart, handsome guy who never tried too hard.

I never let anyone see me sweat. I never turned down a challenge. If I failed at something, I very seldom let people see my display of emotions. I considered myself to be a strong person, so I didn't want to appear weak. I didn't have my parents' shoulders to cry on, so I didn't have much time to feel anything I was going through. I learned, over time, to suppress my feelings. My friends told me that it seemed like I didn't care about much.

The worst part of no one believing I had feelings was that everyone tried to push my buttons, just to see if they actually worked. I really don't know what people were looking for out of me, but I would never display any more than what they had already seen.

From about the age of eight, I remember trying to get my parents' attention about things I did in school; their responses were minimal. I would show them different pictures and art projects that I had done in school, and their reaction was the general response. "Oh, good job, Ricky."

Looking back, I believed I suppressed many emotions because I believed, "If my parents don't care, I will do my best to impress my teachers."

Teachers were the only ones who seemed to like the way I was.

The positive thing that I drew from not having the ability to feel emotions was when I started reading books about the way things were in history, I didn't get so lost in how I felt about what I read.

I took all I could as reference and held it in my mind, so I remembered where my people came from and how they were treated. The mentality that was passed down from generation to generation, and the traditions that were given to African Americans by their masters, including Christianity. There were times when the slave masters used the Bible to control and to manipulate the slaves to behave—obedience meant going to heaven when they died.

Whether or not all slave masters treated their slaves that way, of course, no one could be sure. One thing I believed was that many of them did. The slaves, once they believed they were free, started their own churches with the same level of manipulation and control used on their members.

Church, as I knew it, was a place my dad dragged me to, to do things I never wanted to do. Deep down inside, I never wanted to do anything that didn't feel genuine to me. Singing in the youth choir, going to Sunday school, and memorizing Easter speeches was never something I found appealing.

The ministers and elders walked passed and spoke to one another, but never spoke to me or the other young people. They didn't seem to like the sight of us, and only pretended to admire us during youth Sunday.

I will never forget, one Youth Sunday, I was playing the drums, Reggie was on the organ, and Tiffany was leading the youth choir in a song. Tiffany wasn't the best singer, but she loved to sing. As the choir sang, and Tiffany did her hardest to do well, I saw those ministers and deacons looking at one another, laughing.

I knew, from that point on, this particular church was full of people who didn't really care about anyone. I don't even know why they went to church, other than to socialize.

It looked like that was the reason why my dad was there, that's for sure. He didn't have friends. The church was his friend, and it was his happy place. I felt if I could just be a part of the church, it would make our relationship grow stronger.

As much as I wanted to have a relationship with my dad, I wasn't willing to change who I was to please him. I wanted him to be there for me, without me having to be fake—somewhat like how he loved my mom.

No matter how crazy my mom acted when she was drunk, my dad loved her like I didn't know a person could love another. I didn't see the affection, but I remember seeing my mom in fits of rage, and he would just sit there and take it.

One day I even asked him why he put up with her and all of the drama that came along with her. It wasn't until that day, I realized my mother, Gloria Thompson, was more than just a drunk.

"When I met your mother, she was working at the grocery store, as a cashier. Her smile lit up the entire atmosphere," my dad said to me, with that twinkle in his eye. "There was never I time I went into that store, and she was not pleasant to every customer she came in contact with. We started dating, and as time went on, we fell in love.

"She showed me such love and affection. She even cooked meals for me, did my laundry with me at the laundromat. I had never felt this love from another woman in life. I had girlfriends before her but no one tolerated me the way she did. She was a wonderful woman, and an incredible wife.

Within four months of marrying, we were expecting our first baby. She was on cloud nine, although I wasn't.

"One day, when she was about five months pregnant, she was lifting a box of cans at the grocery store, and her water broke. A few hours later, after a painful delivery, she gave birth to a tiny baby girl who didn't take more than two breaths.

"She fell into a deep depression after that, and I knew this was a test for me to show her I would support her no matter what. After a few years, you came along and we were both so very happy to have you. You were the perfect baby, while you were in the hospital at least.

Once I brought the two of you home and went back to work, your mom suffered from postpartum depression, which led to the drinking. She would go days without eating, and although she was not working, I had to take you down the street to Miss Shirley's house to be cared for.

"I want you to know that your mom's alcoholism has really gotten in the way of many things, but I will never change the commitment I made to her. I will always remember who she was when I met and married her, and I will never turn my back on her. She has no one else, but me and you, so it is our responsibility to love and protect her, no matter what anyone else has to say about her."

The way my dad talked about my mom was amazing. I really admired everything he said to me about his feelings for her. What he described to me was something I knew I wanted to experience with my wife. I believed that I could love a woman that way, if she could love me the way my parents once loved each other.

Although I didn't see or have the privilege of knowing my mom the way she once was, deep down inside, I respected her for the woman she tried to be. I love her for giving birth to me, despite how painful it must have been, every year seeing her original due date pass of her first baby, wondering what it would have been like have a daughter to love and get matching outfits with and getting hair done together.

I began to love my mom in a way I hadn't loved her, previously. Her alcoholism didn't make me want to change her, no more than I wanted anyone to change me. Just as my dad tried his best to love her, I committed to do the same.

My only concern was wondering who would love me the way I needed it.

CHAPTER ELEVEN

THINGS AS THEY SEEMED

Upon graduating high school, I saw my life going exactly in the direction I had planned. I got a full basketball scholarship to Bloomfield College to study business. My mind was completely focused on breaking the cycle of what I saw on display in my parent's household. I wanted to build a life for myself, without having to tell anyone the one thing that my dad told everyone. The first thing he said during successful times was, "Glory to God! God is good!"

Everything that happened in our lives was nothing but the goodness of the Lord. I never understood why things couldn't just be amazing because we actually put forth the effort to do things.

Why was it that we had to thank God for every single thing that we did? Why was it great?

When things went wrong, we were still supposed to thank God. When my mom prematurely gave birth to that baby, I wonder if my dad said, "Well, praise God. Thank you Jesus."

If I were to be thankful to God for anything, or anyone, I would thank God for the stars aligning themselves and bringing Angela into my life. The day I met her was one I will never forget.

I was in McDonald's with a few of my friends from the basketball team, and we were talking about a party we wanted to go to that weekend. Angie was there, alone, but she seemed to have been talking to an older woman she may have known for a long time. They were talking about a church service or something, and I was looking at her, wondering why such a beautiful girl would waste her weekend at church at her age. The older woman left and once I noticed I was clear to talk to Angela, I approached her.

"What's your name, young lady?" I asked her, as I stood there with my arms folded.

"Angela," she said, shyly, as she looked down at the floor.

When I realized she was interested, I pretended I didn't know what was going on.

"My name is Rick, and I would love to spend some time with you, when you're available."

"Okay, but when? I am pretty busy, because I'm in school right now. It's not really easy for me to take much time away from my studies."

"I understand and I respect that. I'm an athlete, and I'm also a college student. Maybe we can study together sometime. What school do you attend, Miss Angela?"

"I go to Bloomfield."

"What? No way! So do I."

"You're lying," she said, with a smile on her face, seemingly excited that she found a new friend.

"Okay, so let's exchange numbers, and when the time is right, we will spend time together, I'm sure. Let's just see what happens."

For some strange reason, she forgot the first encounter. But when we met the second time around in the registrar's office, while I was straightening out some scheduling issues, I made a better impression.

As time went on, we started to see each other, here and there, never getting in the way of our academics. I was extremely attracted to Angela, and I liked the way she carried herself.

She wasn't much of a party girl from what I saw. I only saw her in school, on campus, between classes. We studied together but didn't push more than that. That was something that I needed. The girls I met at parties were loads of fun to be with, but I never stopped thinking about the kind of woman I needed in my life. I fantasized about what my parents had before I was born, and wanted nothing less than that for myself.

By senior year of college, I knew that I wanted Angela to be my wife. I had clearly seen all I wanted to see of women, on and off campus. The way things had changed during my college years made me want to be as grounded as possible. I was very aware of what life had to offer me, if I didn't get right out there and look for a job.

I talked to Angela and made my intentions clear to her, and her parents, on graduation day. We all went out to eat together, because my mom was in the hospital with liver disease, and my dad was by her side the entire time.

Although I understood he needed to be by her side, I hoped he would have surprised me, just once, and showed me that something this big would make him want to show up for me. I didn't know anything could keep him from seeing his only child graduate from college.

Strangely enough, though I was extremely embarrassed and disappointed that my dad wasn't there for me during the most important years of my life, and even more hurt that my mom passed away just as I started looking for my first job out of college, I kept moving forward.

By the time the following September after my graduation rolled around, I had been on so many interviews and taken enough assessments that I felt there was nothing more I could do. I went to my dad and told him I was basically at my wit's end, and I would be staying with him much longer than I wanted to.

He told me how important it was to pray, and that nothing came just by what I was doing.

I tried prayer but nothing seemed to happen for me. Then, one day, my dad told me that someone he knew at the power company was a manager; and if I was looking for a job, I had to be flexible with my work hours.

At twenty-two years old and with a host of ideas for the future, there was no way in the world I would say no to any job opportunity straight out of college.

Going to school, meeting the love of my life, graduating, and now having a decent paying job was something I needed more than anything else in life. I was the happiest man on Earth.

I wasn't happy because I went to church every Sunday, I wasn't happy because I read the Bible, and I know my happiness didn't come from my prayers. I believed my dad prayed a lot for me, so there was no real need for me to pray.

What did I need to pray about? Life was great!

CHAPTER TWELVE

RIGHT OR WRONG?

Marriage was everything I thought I wanted. It eventually turned into a mess of things I didn't want. There were no serious issues from what I could remember. It seemed as though we just did what we had to do and everything else seemed to work out.

The first few years that we were married, I remembered going on dates together, always having someone to help us with the kids, going places we loved. It's not so much that we had everything, but we had one another and nothing else mattered.

Whatever I wanted, Angie found a way to make it happen for me. I remember telling her I wanted to get a 1997 Honda CBR 750, and she gave me her tax refund to get it. It seemed like there was nothing she would not do for me. I knew that I had the right woman for me.

When our children were born, we struggled a little with the night duties of having a little one up at night and a toddler up all day long. We were no different than other people who had small children. We pushed through every issue and never seemed to let our concerns with each other interfere with our financial goals and relationship.

After two children and ten years of marriage, things began to change. Angela said she felt no peace in her life. She told me that she wanted to do things that lifted her up. Since she always supported me, I told her I would support her in what she needed from counseling or anything else she felt would bring her mood up a little more.

As time went on, I saw a gradual change in her life which appeared to make her more positive and willing to move in a direction that made her feel more fulfilled as a wife and mother. She came to me and asked me what she could do to make me happier, but I honestly felt that nothing could have been done to make me feel any better than I did.

We did everything as a family. If Nikki had a dance recital, or Tyler had a soccer game, we figured out a way to support each one of them as best we could. They would do sports that took place in different seasons, so we could be there and teach them how important it was to cheer each other on.

I always wanted my parents to cheer me on during games. That was something I didn't have as a child; I wanted to make sure my children had it. The looks I saw on their faces expressed the excitement I never experienced. It was in those very times that I felt a sense of pride, doing something for my children that my parents never did for me.

Angela expressed strong interest in committing her life to Christ. I told her if that was something she wanted to do, as anything else, I would support her since it was something that made her feel better. I never thought it was a bad idea for anyone to tell another to have spiritual guidance. I always believed that we were spiritual beings, having human experiences.

My personal religious experiences caused me to doubt Jesus. I believe there is a God, so I'm not an atheist. I do believe that He created us to have dominion over the earth. My confusion increased as I grew up in the church I attended with my parents. I never understood the teachings, completely. I also had a hard time believing all the stories we were told.

My question was always, "How do we know these things really happened? How do we know that someone didn't decide to make these things up to manipulate and control us?"

My father often shared so much of the scriptures with me. I knew the basic scriptures that many children learned in Sunday school. I didn't even give thought to what they meant, nor did I really care.

My friends and I were told we needed to keep these scriptures close to our hearts to get through life as we matured and went through the many storms of life.

Reading books about the actual history of the United States drove me further away from what my father believed. I read many accounts on how the Bible was used to control slaves and manipulate them into doing certain things.

The scare tactics used certainly made them want to be the best slaves they could be. These slaves were beaten by people who claimed to preach to them about how important it was to be obedient. The very same people who tore them away from their families, to make them weak, were the same ones who told them that God made them strong, to do the labor.

As I read on and on about the history of the church, it was brought to my attention that many of these churches were founded by people who were born into the traditions of the slave masters. This meant that people were only believing in a God that was said to feel a certain way about them only if they did what His word said.

How could this have really happened this way? How could people really believe that the same people who treated them so badly loved them enough to give them hope to believe in their God?

The more Angela became involved in the church, the more she wanted to go. It seemed that she was on an emotional high every time she came home from church. She told me she never wanted to "leave the same way she went in" as many people said about going to church. She said things like "my church is different" and "we aren't the typical church".

As much as I wanted to believe it, I couldn't understand why I still had similar childhood feelings when I tried to visit church with her. I think my biggest issue was my unanswered questions.

Further involvement in church started causing issues at home with the children. They started asking me where she was on the nights they had games. There were some times they acted like they didn't care, but I knew it bothered them. The normal things we used to do as a family became a thing of the past. She went her own way, and it became something she wanted us to do with her. This church thing was something she was doing alone; but as with most things, a little wasn't enough. She wanted to see us do it as a family.

By the time Tyler and Nikki were six and eight years old, the tug of war between the two of us was serious. Sundays, she would have them going to Sunday school because "they need to

know Jesus for themselves." This was something she said her mother often told her.

I believed what she was saying, in a sense, but I didn't want her forcing all of her beliefs on them. I didn't want her using these teachings and learnings as something to control the children, like her mother did with her. If there was something she wanted to teach them, I understood; I just didn't want her using it for the same reasons the slave masters used it.

The love for my family was not something I wanted to give up, under any circumstances. I wanted my wife and children with me, under the same roof. I didn't want anyone else to be there for my children.

Angela and I had so much history. We had struggled and fought so much to get where we were, financially and emotionally. It seemed that the church was now all that mattered to her. I had no idea how to move forward with her. I wanted to go to Maxwell and Jill Scott concerts and to enjoy ourselves, like we used to.

Was that too much to ask?

CHAPTER THIRTEEN

A DAUGHTER'S ANSWERED PRAYER

The next few months were filled with the most challenging and mind-boggling moments I had ever experienced in my life. There was no real understanding, or explanation, as to why or how everything happened so quickly.

I know what the doctors said. The fact that we were all so unwilling to accept the truth was what made it more difficult. The blockage my mom had was a result of repeated sinus issues never followed up on. She believed and had faith that God would heal her in His time.

Pastor Michael and his wife came to visit every few days, to check on my mom, to ask questions, and to have prayer with her. She wasn't able to talk, and she had to learn how to do the things we basically did without thinking about every day.

Her right side was paralyzed, so she could only move her left limbs. The right side of her face didn't move when she smiled, and her right eye looked a little different than it normally did.

My heart was broken.

Tyler wouldn't enter the room with us for weeks, without crying. I didn't know who I felt worse for. Every time he saw Mom laying there, sleep or awake, he seemed to be overwhelmed and clothed in complete fear of the unknown. Then, he'd start trembling.

Dad was supportive the entire time, like I knew he would be.

I didn't think about how I felt when I looked at Mom. It was like I didn't have feelings when I went in there. I just wanted her to know that I loved her, and I wanted to be by her side. I had no idea what it felt like to have a stroke, to lay in bed, helpless, and not know what would or could happen next.

She knew what happened to her, but she had no idea where this road was leading her.

I wondered if she felt like the Lord was allowing this to happen for a reason. I wondered if she was angry, or if she just thanked God that she was still alive. I didn't ask her because she couldn't respond to questions.

"How are you feeling, Ange? You good?" Dad said to Mom, as he sat on the side of her bed.

"Mmmm," she moaned, with a weak tone.

"The doctor said you did well in the emergency surgery and that you will be able to go to rehab in a few days, as long as you remain stable."

As he said that, a tear rolled down her face. She just stared at my Dad and didn't bother to take her eyes off him for one moment. I saw the pain in her eyes as she looked, almost as if she had a million questions and no one had the answers.

"No, no, babe. Don't cry. I'm here, and I'm not going anywhere. You know that. We are going to get through this, together like we have with everything else that's come our way. Don't worry about it."

"I'm here, too!" I chimed in.

"Me too," Tyler said.

It wasn't nearly as reassuring as I said it; but he said it, nonetheless.

I went over on Mom's right side, reached across her body, and grabbed her left hand; she squeezed my hand.

"I love you, Mom. I'm so proud of you. You're the best Mom anyone could ever have. We are going to come by and check on you as much as we can, okay? Don't worry about anything. We will do our chores and keep the laundry done. Just concentrate on getting better. We will take care of the rest, okay?"

She squeezed my hand again, and I kissed her on the cheek.

Tyler came over and stood on the left side of the bed and kissed her cheek as well. When he put his lips on her face, I saw how he took in a deep breath, as if he wanted to somehow bring her smell home, to comfort him in her absence.

"Alright, guys, let's go home and let your mother get some rest," Dad said, as he stood up and stretched.

He leaned over, whispered something in her ear, kissed her on the cheek, and then put on his baseball cap.

We all looked back at Mom and waved as we walked out the door. She actually lifted her hand and waved, a little.

Once we reached the elevator, I let out a deep sigh and started crying. I couldn't hold it any longer. I wanted so badly to hold it together until we at least got to the Tahoe—or the house even—but I was bursting with anxiety. I was tired of being strong. I felt like my breath was taken away.

I had never, in my entire life, been forced to be without my mother. I felt like we had done something terrible to deserve this. It was bad enough my parents were arguing over who did what and why they were getting a divorce, but then the unimaginable happened. Our Queen, the glue, the prayer warrior, was in the hospital, and we knew she wouldn't be coming straight home.

This was, by far, the worst timing ever!

A week went by, and my mom started getting better, slowly but surely. The only people we saw visiting from the church were the pastor and his wife. None of the church mothers came by. None of the pastor's aide committee members, none of the ushers, none of the choir members, nor anyone from the auxiliaries that she served on showed up.

I started to wonder if my dad told Pastor Michael and his wife not to tell anyone what had happened, but that just didn't make sense to me. He knew that she loved the church and everyone there, and any bit of company would make her happy.

I also assumed my dad wouldn't say anything about the church people, just to prove a point to my mom about how the church people really were. He never believed there were supportive people where my mom worshipped. I recall him saying that if they were really supportive of her and her family they would've let her miss a few church events to spend time with her family.

I honestly never felt like my mom was forced to do anything at the church. She seemed physically tired going after work, sometimes; but she seemed tired even when she was cooking dinner some days. I didn't think she hated to go to church or to cook dinner, she was just tired.

My faith in God started to change as I watched my mother get stronger. I knew that we could pray and God would hear our prayers, but to see it happen, day by day, right before my eyes really lifted my spirits.

We couldn't see her every day because, once she moved to the rehabilitation center, the physical therapy was intense. I missed her, but I knew she was working hard to come home. I wanted her home; yet I knew once she returned, things wouldn't be completely back to normal for a while.

The doctor was positive she would make a complete recovery. How long it would take was not certain. He said at least six to eight months, to be on the safe side. I don't think we cared how long it would take; we just wanted her to get better.

As my faith in God increased, seeing how well my mother was doing, my faith in church people really upset me. I don't know why a month passed and the people who my mom visited—when they were in the hospital, or when going to court with their wayward children, or even when giving her time to just listen to their problems—were completely absent.

They didn't even call the house and leave messages, to let us know she was on their minds or in their prayers. The very same people who jumped and shouted every Sunday—the clergy, the important office holders, the officials—no one called.

I made up my mind to give up on those people who smiled in my mom's face and didn't have anything to say to her at her weakest moments. She didn't do anything to deserve that type of treatment. She was devoted to those people, and it seemed like the loyalty towards her left with the activities of her right limbs.

"Did you tell the people from church not to contact us while Mom was in the hospital?" I said to Dad one evening, on our way home from visiting Mom.

"Are you serious?" he said, seemingly amused at my question.

"Yeah! I haven't seen anyone but Pastor Michael and his wife, over the past month. That doesn't seem strange to you, being that she was always at church?"

"No. It doesn't surprise me one bit. Do I feel bad that your mom has to go through this to see who really loves her? Yes. I told you and your mother countless times about how ridiculous it was for her to run so much for those people.

"I was never against her believing in God. I believe in God, because there has to be something out there, bigger and greater than us, who created this world. Do I believe there needs to be churches to help us recognize who God is? No, I do not. And this right here, what we are experiencing, is exactly what I was trying to say all along. It's not about the people, it's about God.

"I must say, I was angry with your mom and with everything that was going on between us. I remember saying to my friend Rodney, that if there was any way possible God could show us a miracle and bring us back to where we used to be as a family, I would change my behavior toward my wife and my attitude would be one that shows you and Tyler the kind of father and husband I was when we were first married.

"I don't want a divorce! I want my family together. I want to be the way we were before all this church madness happened. I knew my wife was getting sucked in, from the very first revival she attended with her friend Dora.

"Don't get me wrong, she is a very nice woman from what I remember and I actually didn't mind when she visited. I just wanted my wife with me. I didn't hang out with the fellas, unless there was a Super Bowl party or a boxing match I really wanted to see. I loved being at home, and I took pride in being a faithful man. All I wanted was to be something to my family that my father never was to me."

"I understand what you're saying. I really do. I never knew you believed in God."

"I don't know if I ever believed in God as much as I do right now. Until this point in my life, I felt that He never heard my cries for help. I used to ask Him to fix my mom and please make my dad spend more time with us. It seemed like no matter what I said, things didn't change."

"I guess we never know why God allows some things to happen. One of my teachers said there's no such thing as a loss, just a lesson. So maybe your parents weren't all you wanted them to be, but look at how amazing you are as a dad and a husband. You really love us."

"I do, and nothing will ever come between us again. After seeing how close I came to losing my wife, I will try harder and do more to show her I love her. She will never have to question my love for her again. That's my word."

I noticed a change in my parents as time moved on. Some things I never witnessed before, for obvious reasons. This was a very different situation from anything we ever saw as a family.

The same mom who was always on the go, started to change and get more comfortable with being with her family.

Even as I saw her strength increase, where she was able to walk on her own and get full sentences out, she put more effort toward being with my father and making sure he was happy.

He didn't want her to cook as often as she did prior to the stroke, but that was one of the things she did to balance her time spent at church. We could never say we didn't have a delicious, hot meal on the table every day. That's who she was.

As time progressed, we grew closer as a family, in whatever we did.

My father began to read books on spirituality, the awesomeness of God, and how our relationship with Him molded and positively changed our outlook on life.

I overheard the conversation between my parents about God and how important prayer and fasting was, on a regular basis. They would be in the room for hours just having deep discussions and encouraging each other with different aspects of their spiritual walks. I really loved to see them talking and bonding on a level I had never seen before.

I often wondered if my dad would ever bring us all to church as a family, after his spiritual outlook changed. I didn't want to ruin any expectations, or cause any issues, by asking. I figured it would be much better to wait it out and see what happened.

Three months had passed since the stroke, and we still hadn't seen any members of the church. The pastor and his wife called and sent cards, but even those gestures had vanished after they saw the improvements in my mom's condition.

Pastor Michael and his wife were the nicest people I knew, and I wanted to believe that they really cared about us; but strangely enough, I felt like we were rejects.

I fought the urge to say anything to my mom. I didn't want her feelings hurt. I always saw her as a strong faithful member and a great asset to the ministry. I believed she noticed that I was emotionally affected by what was, and was not, taking place due to the change in attendance after the stroke.

"You know, I had the stroke three months ago, this coming Tuesday?"

"I honestly don't remember the exact date. Was it August 8th?"

"I thought you said you didn't remember," Mom said, with a smile. "We have been through so much as a family, and I believe we all grew through this entire ordeal, don't you?"

"Yes, I really do believe things have changed our lives and made us see things completely differently—in a good way, of course. It seems like you're doing well enough to go back to church. It seems like Dad has been talking to you a lot about God and how much it makes a difference to pray and have faith."

"I see that man in a way that I have never seen him before, Nikki. He is so much more to me than I ever noticed. He has grown in so many ways. I knew your father loved me. It wasn't until I began to pray, and really ask God for understanding as to why He allowed me to have this stroke, that I understood the importance of a real marriage and a real relationship with God.

"I initially thought I was being punished for what had happened. I was wondering where I had gone wrong in my walk with God that I would fall ill at a time when my husband no longer wanted to be in the same house with me. We walked past each other with such disgust, without one concern about how it made you and Tyler feel. We were equally selfish and inconsiderate of you children that we were raising to love and support our family.

"I apologize to you for that. It wasn't fair at all what I did to you. I apologize for not supporting you in the areas where you needed me most. You were trying to open up to me about your friends and relationships, and I stood from a judgmental place rather than a place of love and refuge.

"I was doing what I thought was best, at the time. I know now that I need to do better for you and Tyler. I can do better, and I will!

"Psalm chapter 133, verse 1 says, 'Behold, how good and how pleasant it is for brethren to dwell together in unity!' Life has become so much better because we have all decided to find balance.

"Ecclesiastes chapter 3, verse 1 says, 'To everything there is a season, and a time to every purpose under the Heaven.' I recognize the season we are in, now. God got my attention. I know what time it is. I need more of HIM, not to be obsessed with being recognized in the pulpit."

Tears began to roll down my face, as I finally saw my own personal prayer about my family being answered. It was not about the church. It wasn't about my attendance, or singing in the choir, or being on the praise and worship team.

My life's strong foundation was built on my personal relationship with God. The way I felt during the worst time in my life was the actual season that brought my entire family closer to God. At the time when I thought God didn't hear my prayers, and I wanted to stop praying, I remembered this scripture I learned in Sunday school, years ago.

"Rejoice always, pray continually, give thanks in all circumstances; for this is God's will for you in Christ Jesus." (1 Thessalonians 5:16–18, NIV)

My mother continued to spend time with us as a family and occasionally went to church with her friends, visiting for different events and services; but she didn't return to the level of attending services like before. She seemed to be at peace with her decision to keep her family first, because of all the time she had spent in church for the last ten years.

I never believed my mom's relationship was any more real outside of church than in the church. I felt like her validation no longer needed to come from the pulpit. It was within herself, and with my father, her husband, the love of her life.

I know she continued to love God with all her soul, and no one would ever change that. Seeing my parents reading the Bible together and inviting us to sit with them to read scriptures and discuss our own understanding of the Word increased our faith even more.

We gradually became the family my mother had always prayed for. God didn't answer her prayer the way she thought he would, but we knew for sure it was answered. There was no denying that.

I think my dad tried to get us to understand his point as well. He had a rough childhood, and his faith was shattered by the things he experienced over the years; but God brought him right back to the place where he belonged.

He was the head of the house, showing us that he and my mom were one and they did the most important things together. They not only raised a family and did the work of building an amazing life for themselves, they grew in their relationship in God and showed us how it was supposed to be done.

They showed us through prayer and fasting, reading God's word, and loving one another.

Every day wasn't perfect, and we didn't expect it to be; but the constant love and support was there. We felt it both ways, and nothing could change what we thought and felt for God and our parents. We were of one mind; we all believed. We weren't so full of excitement that our mother wasn't at church all the time, because we knew she enjoyed it. We were more grateful to be given a second chance, after the stroke, to appreciate one another more.

We watched God perform a miracle on our parents' marriage. He gave us what we needed to remember that He was the One who gives and takes away.

I believed that one day we would all go to church as a family, when Dad was ready. We didn't know what church and what Sunday.

Mom said she would continue to pray and watch God continue His good work in him. I had no other choice but to understand and to agree, after all we had experienced.

Dad surprised us with a mini vacation for Labor Day weekend. We hit Point Pleasant beach, strolled up and down the boardwalk and had some fresh lemonade. Tyler certainly enjoyed the view of all the girls in bikinis. The weather was perfect; we had a great time.

From that point on, I decided to just enjoy what was left of the summer and to prepare for my senior year of high school. I knew it would be something I would never forget. I was finally where I wanted to be, emotionally, and I wanted my parents to see me at my best.

I knew that I could do anything with God on my side.

www.ingramcontent.com/pod-product-compliance
Ingram Content Group UK Ltd.
Pitfield, Milton Keynes, MK11 3LW, UK
UKHW022222230426